PRAYER BOOK
SAINT CHARBEL

PATRON OF THOSE WHO SUFFER IN BODY AND SOUL

Max Ivanova

Introduction

Youssef Antoun, better known as St. Charbel, born on May 8, 1828 in Lebanon, was a priest who spent many years of his life caring for the sick and helping the most needy people, he was a faithful devotee of the Virgin Mary and when he was 47 years old he isolated himself from the world in the hermitage of St. Peter and Paul, in this way he lived ascetically for some years. Saint Karbel died in the Maronite monastery of Annaya, in the middle of the good night of the year 1898 due to a serious illness that would cause him a paralysis in almost all his body. Saint Charbel was beatified on December 5, 1965 by Pope Paul IV and canonized until 1977, being since that year practically the first catholic saint of Lebanon. St. Charbel is known around the world for the many miracles he performed during his lifetime and even after his death, among them: restoring sight to the blind, curing invalids, healing incurable diseases and many more.

Saint Charbel has devotees all over the world and he is truly a very miraculous saint. Inside the catholic temples it is very common to see the image of San Charbel full of ribbons of various colors, this is because it is a very old tradition that the faithful write down in these ribbons the petitions to this miraculous saint so they would be ready to present them before his presence. Today this tradition is still in force and the fame of Saint Charbel is growing little by little in these difficult times. In Mexico, for example, he is a very venerated and beloved saint.

In fact, on July 24 in some parts of the country the feast day of Saint Charbel is celebrated.

Dear reader, if you wish to know some of the prayers dedicated to Saint Charbel and put them into practice, either out of necessity or simply out of devotion, here you will find a series of powerful prayers frequently used by his faithful for different purposes, they contain an intrinsic power and through your faith, they can be of great help in your life.

The Color Of Ribbons And Its Meaning

Earlier I told you that in the cult of Saint Charbel it is very common to find ribbons or ribbons of different colors, placed inside temples, on religious images of Saint Charbel. These ribbons have the petitions of the faithful written on them and each color has a particular meaning.

White

The white ribbon is used for petitions that have to do with protection and peace in the home, it is also used to thank for a fulfilled petition.

Yellow

The yellow ribbon is used for requests related to school, getting a job and everything related to the intellect.

Green

The green ribbon is used for everything that has to do with health, recovering from an illness, asking for a family member, sick person, etc.

Gold

The gold ribbon is used for requests related to material goods, land problems, debts, money and economy.

Blue

The blue ribbon is widely used for protection, envy, jealousy, slander and betrayal.

Red

The red ribbon is one of the most used for purposes related to love, infidelity, attraction and couple reconciliation.

Purple

The purple ribbon is used for purification purposes in all aspects, physically, emotionally and mentally. It is also widely used to ask for the annulment of a witchcraft work.

Pink

The pink ribbon is often used for problems of enmities, reunions, rebellious children and true love.

NOVENA

Prayer Preliminary

Oh, Almighty GOD!

You alone are infinitely Holy and Glorified by all your angels, you who inspired the holy monk and hermit Charbel to live and die in perfect grace with Jesus, giving him the strength to separate himself from the world in order to make triumph, in his hermitage, the heroism of the monastic virtues: poverty, obedience and chastity, today we implore you to grant us the grace to love and serve you by following his example.

Oh, Lord Almighty!

You who manifest the power of the intercession of St. Charbel with numerous miracles and favors, grant us this difficult and urgent grace which in these difficultgrace that we need so much in these difficult times.

(Say what you wish to achieve with this novena)

We thank you Lord for your great intercession.

Amen.

Day I

Oh, Miraculous Saint Charbel!

Whose pure body emanates the perfume from heaven, come to my aid and ask GOD for the favor and grace of
the one i need so much

(make the request)

If it is for the glory of God and health of my soul.

Oh, Saint Charbel, pray for me.

Oh, Mighty Lord!

You who gave St. Charbel the grace of faith the grace of faith, I (your name)
through his intercession, the divine gift and grace of faith, to live in the fulfillment of your commandments and your Gospel. Glory to You forever!

Amen.

Day II

Oh, Saint Charbel!

Oh martyr of the religious life! You who have experienced suffering and now help all who suffer, for the Lord has made of you a shining beacon, today I turn to you as my light in this need and ask GOD through your intercession for the grace of

(make the request)

I trust you, for I know that you
can get it for me.
can obtain it for me.
Amen.

Oh, St. Cherbel!

Oh, Almighty GOD!

Who has honored Saint Charbel by granting him the grace to work miracles, have mercy on me and please grant me what I ask through your intercession.

Glory to You forever!

Day III

Oh well-beloved father Charbel!

You who shine like a resplendent star in the sky, please, I ask you to illuminate my path, and fortify my hope.

I humbly ask you to
grant me:
(make the petition)

Intercede for me before the crucified Lord, whom you have continually adored.

Oh Saint Charbel!

Example of patience and silence, intercede for me.

Oh Lord GOD Almighty!

You who have sanctified Saint Charbel and helped him carry his cross, grant me the courage to endure the difficulties of life, with patience and abandonment to Your holy will, through the intercession of Saint Charbel, to You be the grace for forever.

Amen.

Day IV

Oh affectionate father Saint Charbel!

Today I turn to you with all the trust of my heart, so that by your powerful intercession before GOD, you grant me the grace that I ask of you:

(make the request)

I ask you to show me your affection once again.

Oh, Saint Charbel!

Great garden of virtues, I beg you: intercede for me

Oh, Lord Almighty!

You, who have granted Saint Charbel the grace to communicate with you, grant me, through his help, to be in Grace with you.

Have mercy on me, so that I can praise you forever.

Amen.

Day V

Oh Saint Charbel, well loved by GOD!

Enlighten me and teach me what I must do to please GOD.

Oh, affectionate father; I beg you ask GOD for grace:

(make the request)

Oh Saint Charbel, friend of the humble, intercede for me.

Oh, GOD, I ask you to listen to my request through the intercession of Saint Charbel!

Lord save my poor heart, and give me the peace that I long for.

Calm the tribulations of my soul, to You praise forever.

Amen.

Day VI

Oh, Saint Charbel!

Mighty intercessor, in everything difficult, urgent and desperate problem, I ask you to grant me what I need so much.

A single word from you to Jesus is enough for Him to forgive me, have mercy on me, and respond to my request, granting me the grace of:

(make the request)

Oh, Saint Charbel!

Joy of heaven and earth, I ask you to intercede for me in this difficult situation.

Oh, GOD Almighty!

That you chose Saint Charbel to implore our cause before your divine power, grant me through his intercession the graces I request, to glorify you with him, forever.

Amen.

Day VII

Oh, Saint Charbel!

Well beloved of all, and help of those in need, I have the firm hope that through your intercession before GOD, I will be granted what I request with faith:

(make the request)

Pray for me glorious Saint Charbel so that my urgent and difficult needs are solved.

Oh, Saint Charbel!

Star that guides the lost, intercede for me.

Oh, GOD, Infinity!
Due to my many sins, I am prevented from reaching your grace.

Lord, bring joy to my sadness heart attending my humble request. To You glory and praise forever.

Amen.

Day VIII

Oh, Saint Charbel!

When I see you kneeling on some simple reeds, or fasting, or mortifying yourself before the Lord, increase my hope and faith.

Therefore, I beg you to help me, so that the Lord grants me the grace that I request:

(make the request)

Oh, Saint Charbel, chosen by GOD, listen to my pleas and intercede for me!

Oh, sweet Jesus, who has raised your beloved Charbel to evangelical perfection, I beg you to grant me to live a life in Grace, according to Your will.

I love you, O GOD my Savior.

Amen.

Day IX

Oh, Saint Charbel!

Here I am at the end of this ninth.
My heart rejoices as you
I speak.

I have full confidence that I will
get from Jesus all that I have
requested by your intercession.

I repent of my sins and
I promise never to fall again.

I ask you to obtain the fulfillment of what I have asked for with my prayer:

(repeat request)

Oh, Saint Charbel!

Crown of glory, bear my petitions and intercede for me
GOD.

Lord, You who hear the prayer of Saint Charbel, and who have granted him the grace to join You, have mercy on me, in my helplessness, save me from all the misfortunes that I cannot bear.

To You be glory, praise, and thanksgiving forever.

Amen.

Prayer to ask St. Charbel For Help

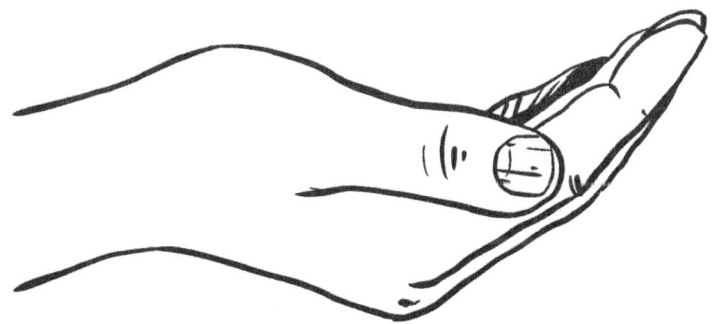

Oh, Blessed Saint Charbel!

That from your holy body you overcame corruption and the perfume of heaven shone on you, today I ask you to come to my aid and grant me the grace that I ask of GOD in this great need that I have today:

(make the request)

Oh Saint Charbel!

Martyr of the monastic life who experienced suffering and for this reason our Lord Jesus Christ made you a beacon of powerful light,

I come to you now and I ask you, for your intercession obtain for me from GOD the grace that I ask:

(Repeat request)

I (your name) trusted your intercession!

Oh, GOD of Mercy!

You who glorified Saint Charbel giving him innumerable graces to perform miracles, have mercy on me and grant me through her intercession the favor that now, I ask you with great faith.

Amen.

Prayer to Thank Saint Charbel

Oh, GOD Almighty!

Merciful and loving,
today, I (your name) bow to you and send you my affections, from the bottom of my heart I send you this prayer of thanks for everything you have given me and will continue to give me through the intercession of Saint Charbel.

That is why I am very grateful to you or admirable Saint Charbel!

Amen.

That I can't find the right words to express my gratitude for the benefit received, for the favor you have given me granted in your great goodness.

Oh, Saint Charbel!

I thank you most sincerely for the help you have given me by sending all my requests to Heaven.

Today I thank you for your intercession and I ask you to continue to assist us in our sorrows; from the Heights where you enjoy your own merits.

Give us your hand and do not let us go, give us your charity, your shelter and protection, when we come to you in despair in our afflictions, help us always and do not leave us in oblivion.

I (your name) in particular, beg you to stay by my side and make me a better person and not faint despite the difficulties, increase my faith and my hope, teach me to have charity with my similar and that I do not depart fromthe teachings of Jesus so that always be worthy of GOD's graces and deserve his favors. So be it. Today and always.

Amen.

Prayer For Love

Oh, holy Saint Charbel.

Today I am addressing you, you who were always alone and who chose the holy church above all else.

I know that after an exemplary life you are now with GOD enjoying his kingdom.

I (your name) come before you to beg you to purify my relationship, which is not going through the best moment.

Oh, holy Saint Charbel.

I long for you to show me the right path, just as you found it within your sacred monastery.

That is why I humbly ask you to advocate for me, before GOD so that with his great power he helps me and removes all the obstacles present in my love life.

Amen.

Prayer for Difficult Cases

Oh, Saint Charbel!

Glorious martyr of life monastic that you retired to a hermitage to live in solitude and to give yourself body and soul to serve the Lord.

You who were honored with the grace to perform miracles and help us in the most difficult problems: today I ask you to come to my aid and please ask GOD to be kind to me and not to abandon me now that I need him so much.

Oh dear father Saint Charbel!

Admirable revered monk and acclaimed by all who during your virtuous and miraculous earthly stay, you did not stop givinghelp, even to the most helpless, alleviating their sorrows and needs of the body and soul now that you are next to the Throne of GOD and from there by your merits you enjoy your own light lend me your great help in my sufferings.

(Mention your request)

To you, who are a prodigious intercessor before the Most High, I want to humbly ask you to approach him with my pleas so that what I ask for is favorable to me. Divine grant me:

(Mention your request again)

Saint Charbel, Oh beloved Saint!

I know I'm counting on you, well my heart is full of trust in you, by the strength of your mediation and for your great generosity, for your love for the Eucharist and the Virgin Most Holy, for your constancy in prayer, fasting and sacrifices, I ask you to never stop advocating for me.

Oh, saint crowned with Glory!

I ask you to lighten the load that I carry on my shoulders, so that the difficulties I go through end, smooth my paths and give me courage and a lot of patience.

Teach me to be a better person, not to sin and not to lose hope in the goodness of GOD
So be it.

Amen.

Prayer To Solve Problems Economic

Oh, miraculous Saint Charbel!

You who are the goodness of heaven, I ask you please, come to my aid
and obtain for me the grace that I need, if it is for the glory of GOD and the good of my soul.

Saint Charbel, pray for me!

Glorious martyr of the monastic life, who tasted the terrible torment of the heart and body.

The Lord Jesus made you a shining beacon, that is why I turn to you to ask for your blessing.

Oh Saint Charbel, pray for me!

Oh Eternal GOD!

that you honored Saint Charbel with the power to achieve great wonders, give me your compassion and grant me what I seek through his powerful intercession.

Glorious Saint Charbel, example of peace, pray for me!

Oh GOD Almighty!

That you honored Saint Charbel with the power to achieve great wonders, give me your compassion and
grant me what I seek for your powerful intercession.

Glorious Saint Charbel, example of peace and silence, pray for me!

Blessed Saint Charbel, garden of virtues, pray for me!

Oh, miraculous Saint Charbel!

Beloved of GOD, help me and teach me to do what pleases GOD and come help me.

Humble Saint Chárbel, friend of the needy, pray for me to GOD and obtain his help so that my financial needs are resolved urgently, listen to my request and save me from this misery, in order to give comfort to my poor heart.

Amen.

To Recover From Illness

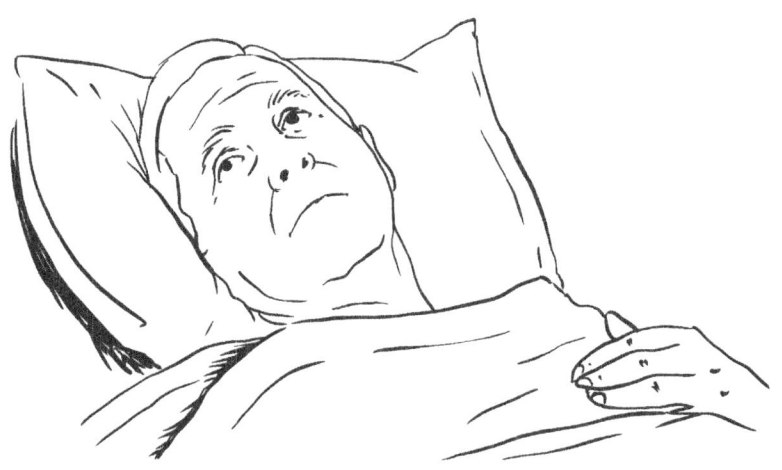

Oh, Jesus Christ, our Lord!

Grant that through this prayer to Saint Charbel, which I humbly dedicate, my soul and spirit may be healed, so that my health may be fully restored!

Oh, Saint Charbel, you who from young man you worked many miracles, holy hermit. protect me and give me, through your extraordinary goodness, the health that I need so much.

Saint Charbel if you grant me this miracle, I (your name) promise to do and follow the path that GOD gives us to save our soul.

Saint Charbel, when you were young in the holy monastery, you granted many prodigals to your friends, that's why I ask you, I beg you and I beg you, to help me take care of my health, and that this disease, which I suffer from today, disappear from my body, completely!

Saint Chárbel, do me the prodigious miracle that for my health, humbly, today I implore you!

Saint Charbel, great saint, in your wonderful goodness I place my faith!

Saint Charbel, most excellent saint, who always advocates for our health and who, even from your holy sepulchre, continues to heal, that there are many who testify in your favor,

I (your name) ask you and beg you, help me with this evil that I can no longer stand!

Please relieve my sorrows, so that my body can rest from so many ills, in exchange I offer you that

stop sinning, enter into prayer and repent of all the evils I have done against the word of the only living GOD!

Amen.

Prayer to Thank Saint Charbel

Oh, GOD of Silence, that in stillness Your adorable and mysterious Trinity lives, loves and acts!

In the silence of time, Your great Mysteries have been fulfilled.

Blessed is he who calms everything within himself and listens to the impetuous voice that leads to You, Saint Charbel heard this voice and shut himself up in solitude.

He separated himself from a selfish world and
He spoke to you, you taught him to deny himself and to die, like a grain of wheat.

You asked him to join you in a life of humility, chastity and obedience, freed from himself, he discovered you.

Oh Lord, he embraced the way of the Cross and filled his spirit with the memory of the passion and death of your Son.

The holy Mysteries became his life, the Eucharist his real food and the Mother of GOD his consolation.

Day and night he searched for you in the scriptures and in the lives of the
Saints.

Through endless prayer, his entire life became a living hymn of Great praise to you and ended in a sacrifice of love that continues to proclaim your glory.

That is why we beg you for his intercession, that you inspire us to a life of prayer and sacrifice. Help us to live lives of tranquility and dedication to the service of Your Church, forever.

Dear Lord, You, who taught Charbel to take root in the monastic vows, who lived in absolute silence and neutrality, conforming his life to yours, helping us to commemorate him and meditate on his extraordinary heroic life by telling him:

Blessed are you, Saint Charbel!

Because in the distant village of your serene family and your relatives you had a passion for prayer, virtue and piety when you were still a child.

Blessed are you!

Because you aimed at the monastic life, accepting the call of GOD in full freedom. Therefore, you left your village Bakafra and never returned.

Blessed are you!

Because you dedicated your life to the monastic vows and to the priesthood, participating daily in the mass and continually and tirelessly looking at the face of GOD!

Blessed are you!

For having shined among the other hermits due to your utter asceticism and unnatural silence that astonished everyone who knew you even after your death!

And now, my Lord, we ask you for intercession of Saint Charbel, may he keep his Church enriched with all those who have a similar life and who follow in the footsteps of our holy priests, hermits and monks who sacrifice themselves for the salvation of the whole world.

Amen.

Prayer To Saint Charbel For Very Difficult Cases

Oh, Glorious Saint!

Blessed Saint Charbel!

Called by GOD to live in absolute solitude, consecrated by love only to Him, and that with penance and austerity, and inspired by the light of the Eucharist, you carried your cross with patience and abandon.

Illuminate our path with your immense faith, and with your encouragement fortify our hope.

Saint Chárbel, beloved son of GOD, who in the hermitage, separated from everything on earth and with authentic poverty and humility, you experienced the suffering of body and soul to enter gloriously into Heaven, teach us to bear the difficulties of life with patience, tenacity and courage, and save us from all the misfortunes that we cannot bear.

Saint Charbel, miraculous saint and powerful intercessor for all in need, for how much you are acclaimed, for being a saint full of love and charity, I come to you with all the confidence of my heart to request your help and protection in this difficult situation, I beg you to grant me urgently the grace that I have so much need today.

(say your request)

A single word from you to your love, Jesus Crucified, our Savior and Redeemer, is enough for Him to take pity on me and respond quickly to my humble request.

Oh, virtuous Saint Charbel!

You who loved the sacred so much eucharist, that you fed on the Word of GOD in the Holy Gospel, that you renounced everything that separated you from the love of Risen Jesus Christ and his Most Holy Mother, the Virgin Mary, do not leave us without a prompt solution, and help us to know Jesus and Mary more and more, so that our faith increases, to serve him better and thus listen to the voice of GOD, to fulfill his will and live from his love.

Amen.

Prayer For the Return of a Lost Love

Oh, Saint Charbel!

Receive this beautiful lighted candle, with the color of the blood that, for love of us, Jesus Christ our Lord, shed on his Calvary.

Before your venerable presence I pray, every day, so that by your miraculous portent, you make (name the loved one) return, I already love him sincerely and without him (her), my soul walks in this desolate world.

Oh, Saint Charbel!

Intercede for me before the Lord
so that he returns to me
(name of loved one)
whom I love so much.

Saint Charbel you who constantly spoke of your love for our Lord Jesus Christ and of your immense love for the Blessed Virgin Mary.

I ask you with great humility to listen to this prayer, to help me return my only love whom I love so much.

Oh, Saint Charbel!

I beg you to grant me one of your numerous miraculous, so that through your immense kindness, I can end this loneliness every day invades my heart.

Amen.

Prayer To Ask For a Sick Family Member

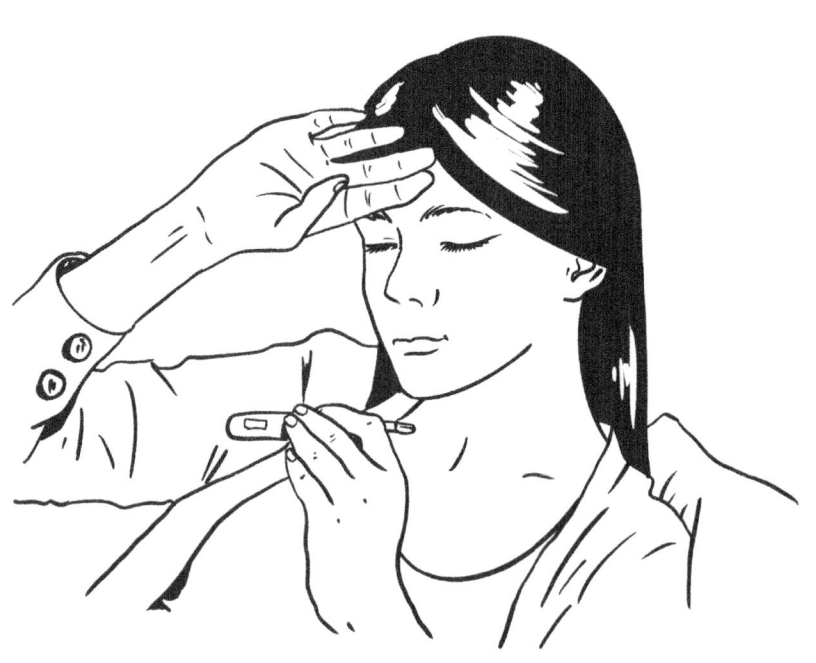

Oh Lord, Father and my God!

You who never desire the death of the sinner, since your mercy has no limit.

That is why today I come to you because you are a kind Father and you love your children beyond borders, forgiving and granting life.

Please, I ask you to deign to accept the sufferings and anguishes, the sufferings and sufferings of your son

(say the name of the sick person)

Since today you are afflicted by pain and illness.

I (your name) ask that through the intercession of Saint Charbel, apostle of the sick, that I always lead an earthly life worthy of you and your works, and for that he deserved your favor and your grace, when after his death I come to your lofty presence, listen to my plea and show us your mercy, granting him courage and patience in sickness.

(say the name of the sick person)

Since today you are afflicted by pain and illness.

I (your name) ask that through the intercession of Saint Charbel,
apostle of the sick,
listen to this humble plea
and show us your mercy, granting him courage and patience in this disease.

If it is your will, beloved Father, grant him the health of the soul and body, manifesting your Great Power of love and compassion, so that healthy and happy he fulfills all your commandments and proclaims your wonders.

Oh Lord!

God Almighty!

Allow your beloved servant, St. Charbel, who works in favor of (say the name of the patient)

So that with the gifts that you have given him, he restores the health of his soul and as well as his body.

And you, dear Saint Charbel, show us once more
your immense charity towards your neighbor, your absolute kindness towards sick people, your great generosity with humanity, your sublime humility and compassion, your great healing and transmuting power.

In order to change the disease for full health, free of suffering, to change the miserable life of your devotee full of sorrow and pain in a life full of strength, well-being and harmony!

Because that's how you did it in life and you continue to do it in the glory of GOD, with humility and kindness without limits.

To you be the Glory now and for ever and ever.

Amen.

Prayer To Saint Charbel To Get A Job

Oh, GOD infinitely Holy and Glorified!

In the midst of your saints, you who have granted to Saint Charbel a great love for the monastic rule, where prayer and work are the only source of holiness, that is why I (your name) beg you through his intercession for the grace to sanctify myself in the search for a decent work.

(make the request)

Oh, Saint Charbel!

I ask you to intercede for me so that I can get a good job, where I can fulfill myself as a person and get enough to support my family.

Keep it despite the adverse circumstances and people.

That in it I progress, improve and hallow.

Amen.

Prayer To Saint Charbel For Love

Oh, Saint Charbel, honorable Saint!

Beloved being that in this life earthly you gave yourself in soul, mind, body and spirit to love Our Lord Jesus Christ.

I ask you, with a humble heart, that you allow me to find joy, peace and much love, that wherever I go, alone or with my family, I find love, affection and the sincere warmth of good friendships, Saint Charbel I ask you to intercede before the Virgin Mary, so that she prays for me and so I can find the love that accompanies me for the rest of my life.

Oh Saint Charbel, you who loved Jesus Christ so much!

As well as all the saints and the Blessed Sacrament.

You who worked so hard for love, that you showed so much love since you were a child, grant me the miracle of finding my great love, so that he may be with me for the rest of my days, and give me, GOD,

Almighty through our Lord Jesus Christ your sacred blessing!

I beg you, even more, I beg you, dear Saint Charbel that you accept this prayer, which I constantly dedicate to you.

Amen.

Prayer To Get Urgent Money

Oh, Lord Most High!

Creator of the universe, to whom belong all the material wealth of this world and even more the spiritual ones, who put and remove kings, I ask you, I beg you and I beg you, with this prayer to Saint Charbel, that you allow me to obtain money urgently, to fulfill this need

(say your need)

Because in this world nobody lends me and I can no longer with this problem, help me Saint Chárbel, you who are Holy, miraculous and kind.

That is why I come before your eternal grace, Lord Jesus Christ!

My Redeemer, I come supplicant through this prayer to St. Chárbel, in which I beg to have the lawful and necessary means to get money urgently
So I can solve this, which only disturbs the holy peace of my home, and is ruining my health, Lord Jesus Christ, I beg you to listen to this prayer to Saint Charbel, since what I require is urgent, Saint Charbel, I thank you.

Amen.

Dear readers, we have reached the end of this book, but not before telling you that Saint Charbel is undoubtedly a highly revered saint in different parts of the world and this is due to the large number of miracles that he has granted to his faithful, if you perform Do these prayers with great faith and you yourself will be a faithful witness of its power. I am Max Ivanova, until next time!

The End

Image Reference

Image Pag.14
Source: https://pixabay.com/es/vectors/virgen-mar%c3%ada-bebe-jesus-l%c3%adnea-arte-5147245/
Image Credits: "GDJ"

Image Pag.46
Source: https://pixabay.com/es/vectors/cupido-eros-griego-amor-mito-1295027/
Image Credits: "OpenClipart-Vectors"

Image Pag.78
Source: https://pixabay.com/es/vectors/personajes-de-historietas-beso-amor-2026849/
Image Credits: "OpenClipart-Vectors"

Image Pag.46
Source: https://pixabay.com/es/vectors/cupido-eros-griego-amor-mito-1295027/
Image Credits: "OpenClipart-Vectors"

Image Pag.99
Source: https://pixabay.com/es/vectors/jes%c3%bas-cristo-l%c3%adnea-arte-adivinar-4033169/
Image Credits: "GDJ"

Printed in Great Britain
by Amazon